LITTLE PATRIOT BOOKS™

When Your Mom Goes to War:
Helping Children Cope with Deployment and Beyond

Maryann Makekau
with
2030north Studios

Also available: When Your Dad Goes to War:
Helping Children Cope with Deployment and Beyond

For information, address:
Maryann Makekau
PO Box 2021
Fort Walton Beach, FL 32549
author@thelittlepatriotbooks.com

Set in Kristen ITC 12 point. Includes references.

LITTLE PATRIOT BOOKS™

When Your Mom Goes to War:
Helping Children Cope with Deployment and Beyond.

Library of Congress Cataloging (Pre-assigned Control Number)
Makekau, Maryann

ISBN-13: 978-0-9826601-9-5
ISBN-10: 0982660197

FOREWORD

Military families know that change is a way of life. It begins with leaving home for basic training. But when Mom goes to war to serve in a foreign land under particularly dangerous working conditions, changes on the home front are more dramatic.

When Mom goes to war, separations are often longer, daily routines are significantly altered, and stressful, intimidating feelings emerge. Mom and every family member require greater support, understanding, and love. New coping tools are needed.

Reading this book together as a family is a great place to start. It offers wonderful ideas of things to do—encouraging everyone to talk, ask for help, share feelings, create positive memories, and "play" as if you are in Mom's shoes. "Doing" helps us not become the "victim" of a deployment; instead, we can use this time as an opportunity to turn it into a valuable life experience.

When Mom goes to war is a time when we can show gratitude for Mom's significant role. It is more than a job! She volunteered to serve a most important purpose - protecting and defending the rights and security of her family, community, and nation. This book lets the entire family know they, too, are serving at home. Everyone is helping to establish Mom's legacy. While Mom may be your *champion*, her military service makes her a great *patriot* and *hero*. She makes us all proud!

LORRAINE K. POTTER
Chaplain, Major General, USAF Retired

BRIEF COUNSEL

The reality is that Moms do go to war, and the resulting separation for a child can seem like an eternity—no matter what age the child. When prepared ahead of time for difficult events like this, emotional distress can be kept to a minimum. In her Little Patriot Book™ When Your Mom Goes to War, Maryann Makekau does just that. As seen through the eyes of a child, Maryann addresses this very heavy issue with insight and charm, using language that every child will understand, amplified by humorous and endearing illustrations.

Children often lack the vocabulary necessary to adequately articulate their thoughts and feelings. Typically they haven't developed coping strategies to deal with such powerful life issues, such as deployment and separation. Without positive coping strategies, children may develop separation anxiety and depression; at times accompanied by acting out behaviors such as regression into an earlier stage of development, aggressive behaviors towards siblings, and oppositional behavior toward caretakers and teachers.

Maryann takes an experience which often makes children secondary victims of the war effort and reframes it so that they instead may become valuable helpers and partners with their moms. Children and parents are empowered by this Little Patriot Book™, through a "toolbox" of ideas to use as they move through such an emotional time.

Not only is this book applicable for children of those deployed, but also for those in any difficult situation involving upheaval, loss, anxiety, and other common emotions. Clergy, teachers, counselors, grandparents, and others would benefit from the tools Maryann gives to help children—they're a remarkable asset in helping families navigate during rough seas. Through this Little Patriot Book™, readers will realize with certainty that indeed "home stays right in your heart." Whether during uncertain times or stable times, that's a significant message to help families maintain faith, love and hope.

CAROL MURPHY, LMHC, RN
St. Simon's Counseling Center
Fort Walton Beach Florida

DEDICATION

Every experience, whether positive or negative, shapes our lives. Although we don't always get to choose the experiences, we do get to choose how we respond to each one. While traveling to share my Little Pink Book™ series to help families cope with cancer, my heart was drawn to another difficult journey numerous families are going through: deployment. Whether I was grabbing a meal, sitting on a plane or at a book signing—the troops readily shared their stories of deployment and its impact on their families. Their stories resonated with me and pressed upon my heart.

Communicating about difficult topics such as cancer, deployment and war is sometimes overwhelming for adults. Answering the questions and concerns of children can be even more complex. Without the vocabulary to express difficult emotions, children tend to simply emulate the adults around them. When unwanted stress from deployment emerges, positive coping strategies are a necessary remedy towards insight and solutions.

These Little Patriot Books™ are dedicated to those children—the little eyes that are watching and learning how to cope. Every soldier who is voluntarily serving our nation and protecting our freedoms, while humbly labeling it all, "just doing my job" became my motivation for writing these books.

As a veteran and career military spouse, raising children amidst transition was a way of life for my family. Transitioning from military service to psychology—as advocate, researcher and author afforded me the opportunity to bless other's lives. When Your Dad Goes to War and When Your Mom Goes to War is one such blessing; it's an honor to provide these titles for the military families engaged in war.

I'm grateful for the numerous interviews with the troops, their families, and to all the military organizations and advocates who opened their doors and their hearts to help me gain crucial insight. A special note of thanks to: Erica, Al, Marissa, Alan, Tina, Willis, Andrea, Deidre, Donald, Jason, Erin, Christopher, Natalie, Krissy and Mary.

Thank you to my family, friends, foreword writers and endorsers for contributing to my work. Thank you to my editor, Amaryllis Sánchez Wohlever, MD for tireless reviews. Thanks to my artist Derek, for the gifts you bring to my life and to these Little Patriot Books™. God bless our soldiers for the freedoms we have due to their sacrifices—may we never forget.

TABLE OF CONTENTS

PACKING FOR CHANGE

What is war? What does war look like? Why does my mom have to fight in a war? Who is she fighting and why are they fighting? These are all questions you might have about war. During war, bad guys do bad stuff like destroying lives, homes, schools, jobs and hospitals.

When soldiers from around the world come together, the good guys (our troops) work hard to fix all the bad stuff! Families get help and injured people get well—but there's A LOT of work to do. The troops, including your mom, are working hard to help heal the countries destroyed by war. Thousands of very brave men and women serve as troops when we go to war, and they all work together to keep our country safe!

If you've lived around the military, you've probably heard some of these words: armored tanks, fighter planes, battle gear, combat boots, chem-gear, dog tags, unit, battalion, mobility, soldiers, deployments, rotations, sorties, Iraq, Afghanistan and insurgents. If your mom going to war is a new thing in your life, it might sound like a whole new language! Not knowing something is just an opportunity to learn. So break out the dictionary or the computer or ask your Mom! Whether riding in the car, choosing a bedtime story, helping your mom pack or all of the things in between—ask questions!

Did you know that soldiers get a "deployment checklist?" Deployment is a big word that means to do your job in a different place! The checklist is really long and it's all written down so your mom won't forget anything! Going to war requires very important items and your mom has to pay close attention to everything she needs to do. Before you know it, her supplies and bags might take over the living room! It takes lots of energy to get ready for deployment.

You can help your mom by asking for your own deployment checklist or you can use the Little Patriot's Checklist in this book! You can get things done faster by asking others for help. The best part of helping out is that you get to be a part of the journey! Although you can't go with your mom, when you help her pack you become part of her deployment right from home.

Whether you're staying in your own home during your mom's deployment or staying somewhere else—home stays right in your heart. Home is the place that everyone remembers and never forgets! Your mom will make sure that no matter who you stay with or where you go you'll have everything you need just like at home.

HUNKER DOWN

Once your mom finishes everything on her deployment checklist, it's time to get ready for the long months apart. If she has a little time before she leaves, maybe you can pick one very special thing to do with mom. You can try to have the attitude of a patriot—how you handle change is very important. You don't have to like the change and you might even feel angry about your mom leaving, but since it's not something you can stop you have to hunker down! That means you have to "hug the new stuff" that's about to happen.

Your imagination can help at times like this. Imagination can take you places! If you've ever played a game on the Wii™, you know just what that feels like! When you play a video game it's like you become a part of it. It's sort of like that when your mom goes to war—you know you can't go with her but you can imagine what it's like to be there.

You can ask an adult to help you put up a world map and "map out" where your mom's going; then draw a yellow ribbon right there on the map! Yellow ribbons are a way for people to show their support of the troops. Mapping out where your mom's going is like following her without leaving your house. Sometimes a deployment is Top Secret so your mom won't be able to say where she's going. This can be fun too because you get to imagine that she's anywhere!

Another great way to experience where your mom's going is to try on her gear before she packs. Playing dress up can make you feel like you're in her shoes! Have you ever put on her shoes and walked around the house in them? They're so big; you have to be careful so you don't fall down! You can even ask to try on her chem-gear, combat boots, dog tags or fleece.

Remember to be very careful and let her help you because her gear is really, really important! Take pictures too—one for you and one for mom. You can keep it by your bed for a heart-goodnight. A heart-good-night is when you can't say "good night" in person; you can say it in your heart instead!

Make a circle of strength by joining hands with your family, saying a prayer or having a big group hug! Changes made with hope and love bless families with strength and courage—and that's the best way to hunker down.

SEE YOU LATER

Saying goodbye can be easy to do when you're going to play with a friend or leaving for a day at school. But saying goodbye when it's for a much longer time is not the same thing at all. It seems like no matter how much you prepare for it, actually doing it is different than you thought.

Whether you've thought it over in your mind or choose not to think about it at all, when it's time for your mom to deploy, you'll have to say "see you later." You've got mom's love in your heart, you've helped her pack, you've done the group hug and yet, you still might not be ready to say goodbye.

Being apart is a big deal for everyone in the family. You can practice ahead of time by hugging often, drawing pictures for your mom and taking on new chores before she leaves. Sometimes, practicing makes things easier. It's sort of like practicing before a baseball game; you're more ready for the game when you already know how to play.

Even though saying goodbye isn't fun like playing a game, it's still something you have to do. Sometimes goodbyes bring lots of tears, hugs and kisses or saying special things like "I love you" and "see you later." But sometimes goodbyes are filled with silence—it's like no one knows quite what to say. Any of those goodbyes are okay. Just make sure you don't miss out on saying see you later alligator!

RED WHITE AND BLUE AND FEELINGS IN BETWEEN

Feelings are like the colors of the rainbow because there are some that are really bright and bold while others are hard to see. Red is one of those colors that really get your attention, like a fire hydrant or a stop sign. Have you ever been so mad that you "see red?" That's one of those adult sayings. It's like when you work super hard on your homework and then you lose it before school! It gets you so mad that you see red!

Adults get mad and frustrated about things too, and they feel red just like kids do sometimes. It's okay if you get really mad at times as long as you don't stay that way. It's no fun to be around somebody who's mad all the time.

happy   sad   angry

Have you ever heard an adult say that they're "blue?" Blue is one of those feelings that are a little harder to see and can be even harder to talk about. It's that feeling when everything seems to go wrong or when your best friend moves away, when you feel like crying. Having your mom deploy might make you red-faced mad or blue-faced sad or even scared.

Scared is a dark color, a feeling that something bad will happen, or how you feel when you wake up suddenly from a bad dream. You try to go back to sleep, but all you can think about is your bad dream. Climbing out of bed for some milk and cookies or snuggling with someone safe can give you good thoughts and help you get back to sleep.

Calm is like the color white, like when you're playing quietly or reading a good book. Pink is a good color for smiling and purple is for riding your bike, and perhaps you're feeling yellow when you add a new ribbon on the map!

Talk about all of your feelings whether you're happy, scared, angry, sad, frustrated or confused! If you're feeling red, white or blue or somewhere in between, it's very important to share your feelings with others. You can talk about your feelings and you can even draw them. Just draw your face, add your color, and tape it on your bedroom door—then everyone in your family will know exactly how you're feeling, especially on tough days.

scared

frustrated

confused

It's always important to let your feelings out so that you can feel better and move on with other stuff, like playing and having fun! Write down some of your feelings to share with mom because talking on the phone or Skyping™ might be really short.

Skyping™ is sort of like being on television but you get to hear and see each other! You can also write letters, make cards, draw pictures, and talk on the telephone. Deployed parents get homesick too, so talking to you and getting mail from you will really help your mom a lot!

HOPE MATTERS

Hope is something you can't touch or see, but you know it's real because you can feel it. It's the feeling that says "no matter what, everything's going to be okay." It's the amazing things that happen that just don't seem possible. Hope says "yes" when it looks like "no way!" Hope is like sunshine inside your heart; it's that bright spot that shines when life seems too hard! Hope matters because it gets people through tough times—sort of like prayer.

Making a "Hope Box" can help you remember to stay hopeful. You can turn an old shoe box into a Hope Box; you can save special notes, cards or pictures from your mom, friends, dad or grandpa. You might get hopeful reminders from lots of people who love you.

One thing that you won't want to save is your worries. Hanging onto your worries is like wearing mom's big shoes—it gets hard to keep going! You might worry, "what if my mom gets hurt or dies?" Be sure to talk about what you're thinking—you're probably not the only one with those worries.

Look through your Hope Box every so often. Some things will make you smile. Other things will spark your imagination. Your friends might want to know about your Hope Box because hope matters to everybody, and hope is contagious—it's catchy!

MISSING IN FAMILY ACTION

One of the hardest things about your mom being deployed is having her miss out on the family action. Family action is all the stuff your mom's usually there for—helping you with Math or being at your music recital or soccer game. A big sister might miss mom's help to pick out the perfect prom dress. A big brother might miss mom's opinion about the cute girl he's eyeing in Gym Class.

While she's missing out on the family action someone has to become the picture taker to help her keep up with all that's going on. You can put pictures in a special book, write notes about them or email them to her over the Internet!

Anytime new things happen, it's always nice to have someone who says just the right thing and their smile makes your day. For a lot of kids that's mom!

On those nights when you're really missing your mom, you can set an extra plate and fork at the dinner table. That lets everyone know that it's a "missing-night." Missing-nights mean it's time for mom-stories around the dinner table. Funny stories, happy stories, missing stories and hug stories! It's fun to set an extra plate for dinner guests sometimes too. Having other people over for dinner creates new stories!

Some kids have a mentor while their mom's at war. A mentor is someone who helps kids when a parent can't be there. Teachers, church leaders, adult friends or family members can all be mentors. Even though no one can ever take mom's place, it's good to have another adult around that you can trust and talk to about anything that's on your mind.

If mom took care of grocery shopping, paying bills, cooking and after-school activities—that's a lot of stuff for a dad to do by himself. The worry of doing all those things can

feel sort of like having a brick on your shoulders. A brick
is very heavy and it can feel like you're carrying one when
you have to do so many things! Even if dad doesn't cook
like mom, tell him "thanks Dad!"

You're not the only one who has lots of things to share-
your mom will be seeing new things while she's away at war.
She'll miss you very much and wish she could share some
things too. Maybe she'll write in a journal, take pictures
or email to share some of the things she's doing; you can
be a part of her deployment action too. Then no one
totally misses out!

JUST LIKE YOU MOM

There are some things that make your mom extra special—maybe she plays your favorite game or helps you learn Math better than anyone else on the planet! Maybe she's a really good listener or a great shopper or perhaps she holds the seat of your bicycle just right so you don't fall over!

While she's deployed, you can do some things just like mom. Ask about getting some camouflaged pajamas, shirts, hats, backpack, or even dog tags. Dressing up and pretending to be just like mom can be lots of fun! And it will help you feel that "heart-goodnight" even during the day!

Praying for your mom while she's at war can help you sleep better by letting go of all your worries. Sleeping better means that you'll have lots of energy to do your school work, help others, play your favorite games and write to your mom! Praying and letting go of worries is helpful for everyone in your family.

You can serve your country by doing all sorts of helpful things just like mom. Serving can include helping with chores at your house, giving a hug to a friend who's sad or helping a neighbor unload groceries. Saying the Pledge of Allegiance or putting your hand over your heart when the National Anthem plays at a baseball game are great ways of serving too.

You can also serve by creating a card station at your house. All you need is a special place in the kitchen to keep some paper and a box of crayons. Anytime someone in your family wants to share something with mom, make a card, draw a picture, write a poem or even make a note for another soldier—just go to the card station to make it in a minute!

HUMOR IN THE MIX

Families talk about lots of things. Deployment and war are very serious things to talk about. Those kinds of talks might make you cry or feel sad. Whether you get in trouble, get a bad grade or a family member or pet gets sick, there can be many other times when families need to have serious talks.

There are also times when humor needs to be in the mix! Some people say that humor is God's best medicine; if you're feeling bad or sad, laughter can make everything better. Doing silly stuff, using your imagination and even laughing 'til you cry, are all ways of putting humor in the mix! In between the serious things, it's really important to have fun.

You can tell jokes or funny stories during car rides. You can talk about those crazy scrunched up faces that mom makes or the silly stuff a brother or sister does! You can play peek-a-boo with a baby and the next thing you know you'll both have the giggles! Get out your favorite board game, make popcorn and enjoy a night of fun—no serious talks allowed!

Invent some new ways of making each other laugh. Try lying down on the lawn at night and giving the stars funny names; then share them during your next phone call with mom or draw a picture to put in the mail! Take turns making silly words out of the letters on license plates you see while stopped at red lights! There are lots of ways to have fun. Adding humor to the mix helps your family get through the tough times and everyone comes out stronger.

23

HOMEWARD BOUND

Group hugs before and after deployment can bring everyone together like a circle of strength. Everyone's had their place in the ranks, doing their part during mom's deployment. Your mom's homecoming is exciting, but it also might feel a little weird—like you're dreaming!

Waiting and waiting is really hard, and now after lots of waiting you finally get to see your mom again. She may be finished with her work at war or she may just be getting a visit between all of the things she has to do there. If her time at home is short, it can feel like it flies by in no time and it might even feel like you've missed out. So it's important to prepare for your mom's homecoming, whether it's short or long.

Finding a place in your house where everyone can write what they want to do with mom can be really helpful. When families are apart, that list can get really long, really fast. You'll have to decide what's most important to you—that way everyone gets a turn and your mom isn't overwhelmed. If your mom has been gone for months and months, it might take a while to share all the things on everyone's list including the things in your Hope Box.

Sometimes, coming home can be weird for your mom too. She might wonder if you'll recognize her since it's been a while. When she sees how much you've grown and all the things you can do without her help, she might feel a little sad too. Be sure to let her know that while some things changed, you still need her for other things. And be sure to remind her of all the things you've missed about her!

Deployment is hard for everyone in the family, but it also makes you appreciate each other more. Your family made it through the tough spots and learned some things along the way. Before your mom's deployment you might have been annoyed by some of the things she said or did, but now you realize you even missed those things! Seeing her again will remind you of lots of the things you've missed. Enjoy a group hug with your family, put some humor in the mix and welcome mom home!

LITTLE PATRIOT'S CHECKLIST

1. Remember that your mom deployed because it's her job. Nothing you did or didn't do caused her to leave to fight in the war.

2. Helping your family while mom is away is one of the most important jobs in the world.

3. Hug others until they let go first; it's really fun to see how long hugs last!

4. Crying is like going through a car wash—when you're done everything looks better and brighter! Everyone needs cleaning like that sometimes. Hugs will help you feel better after crying; they're a gift for the giver and the receiver!

5. Take your Patriot attitude to other places like school, sporting events and church. Your attitude of respect and honesty will encourage others to do excellent things, too!

6. Share your feelings—happy, sad, angry, mad, frustrated or confused. Families are stronger when they can share all those special feelings with each other.

7. Have fun. Play often. Laugh a lot. Use your imagination. Explore the outdoors. Eat well. Stay strong. Love others. Pray for the troops.

8. Remember that as a Little Patriot, you're serving our nation, too. Keep an attitude of gratitude—give thanks for the troops, their families, and freedom!

TIPS FOR FAMILIES

1. Forgetting some things over time is normal. To help your child remember mom during deployments, make time to look at photos, talk about good times, and talk on the phone or Skype.™ Even brief moments of sharing help keep memories intact.

2. Encourage each other to flow with the changes brought on by deployment. Change is an inevitable part of life, although some take longer to adapt than others. Resist the tendency to compare and always celebrate individual milestones.

3. Create a convoy of helps. Asking for help isn't a sign of weakness; it shows that you know your own limits. Make a list of things mom usually does so that when others ask to help, you can simply let them choose from the list.

4. Have a practice run. If mom gets advanced deployment notice, start using some of the tips in this book and others that your family creates. It will allow mom to focus on preparing for deployment and help your family adjust to things being different, even before she departs.

5. If possible, meet with the principal and school teachers prior to mom's departure. Explain how deployment will affect your family and share some of your family's needs- from watching your child for signs of distress to understanding absences, and more.

6. Engage children as much as possible in the deployment journey: helping mom pack, mailing treats, having two kitchen clocks for each time zone and creating a welcome home banner. Keep activities age-appropriate and minimize media coverage that may be biased or too graphic.

7. If your child is withdrawing, crying frequently, becoming aggressive or showing other problem behaviors be supportive and understanding. Reach out for professional help if you don't see signs of improvement.

8. Pass it on. If mom has gone to war before, share what you've learned with families new to deployment. Also share important things you've learned with teachers, church staff, coaches, friends and relatives—anyone who frequently spends time with your child.

9. If a mentor is involved during deployment, help your child transition afterwards so that they won't feel conflicted about sharing time with mom and their mentor.

10. Worrying isn't a job—you don't get paid for it! Avoid spending time worrying about what hasn't happened or what you can't control. Pray and let go; spend time everyday being thankful.

TIPS FOR EDUCATORS

1. Be aware that the vast majority of military children don't live on military installations; they are an integral part of civilian communities. They don't stand out like their parent(s) in uniform.

2. Keep in mind that some children stay behind with a non-deployed parent, while others live temporarily with a relative or family friend. Some children even have to relocate during a parent's deployment—thrusting them into different homes, classrooms and communities.

3. If a new student shows up at school, ask questions and give extra support perhaps through a buddy arrangement, follow up phone calls and caregiver-teacher meetings.

4. Arrange extra support for any child whose parent is deployed, whether or not the child has relocated, and no matter how many times a parent deploys—every deployment is difficult.

5. Encourage other students to show support for parents' military service; involve the classroom in letter-writing and card-making campaigns for the troops.

6. Invite returning troops into their child's classroom. Encourage them to share age-appropriate parts of the deployment journey so that other students can identify with a soldier's lifestyle and sacrifices too.

7. Be watchful for tearfulness, anxiety, acting out, comments or drawings that are worrisome or other problem behaviors that may indicate an emotional toll from parental absence.

8. Be mindful of political views, news stories, and areas of study; honor the troops (student's parents) by monitoring what is shared in the classroom.

9. Encourage patriotic pride by engaging students in marked calendar events that honor our nation and our troops.

10. Consider arranging a small support group with the school counselor for students whose parents are deployed—giving them an opportunity to share with others who are going through the same things.

HELPFUL RESOURCES AND LINKS

References used in this publication:

• Military Officer Magazine, April 2010, "War Hits Home" article by Ellen N. Woods.
• http://www.military.com/benefits/resources/deployment/your-children-and-separation
• www.MilitaryOneSource.com
• http://www.airforcetimes.com/family/military_kidstress_tips_070904w/

Other Helpful Resources and Links:

• www.nmfa.org
• www.militaryChild.org
• www.deploymentkids.com
• www.militaryonesource.com
• http://uso.org/uso-united-through-reading.htm
• http://www.militaryfamily.org/our-programs/operation-purple/
• www.yellowribbon.mil
• http://www.operationwearehere.com
• Hearts Apart Programs
• Airman and Family Support Center
• Army Community Services
• Fleet and Family Services

JOURNAL

JOURNAL

_____

_____

_____

_____

_____

_____

_____

_____

_____

_____

_____

_____

_____

_____

_____

_____

_____

_____

_____

_____

_____

_____

CPSIA information can be obtained
at www.ICGtesting.com
Printed in the USA
276828LV00004B